The Crooked Circle Confluence of Poetry, Round 1

Crooked Circle Press™

Bailey, CO / 2025

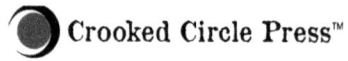 Crooked Circle Press™

The Crooked Circle Confluence of Poetry, Round 1: © 2025 Crooked Circle Press.

Individual Poem Copyrights:

* "The Audition" © 2025, Jenine Baines
* "Apartment for Rent—No Poets?" © 2025, Jenine Baines
* "Sad Toeholds" © 2025, Jenine Baines
* "Moments & Opportunities" © 2025, Jenine Baines
* "Surprise Symphony from Bob, the Music Reviewer" © 2025, Jenine Baines
* "Lift Off at LA Zoo" © 2025, Jenine Baines
* "How to Exit the Body Gently" © 2025, Allisonn Church
* "Apparitions" © 2023, Allisonn Church
* "Waxwing Season" © 2025, Allisonn Church
* "Waterbird and the First Poem" © 2025, Allisonn Church
* "A Feather" © 2025, Allisonn Church
* "Men invented death but women invented soup" © 2025, Allisonn Church
* "The Origin of Wind" © 2024, Allisonn Church
* "Unrequited" © 2024, Allisonn Church
* "Brasso" © 2022, David S. Cohen
* "Fluff and Fold" © 2023, David S. Cohen
* "Recline" © 2023, David S. Cohen
* "Smokestack" © 2023, David S. Cohen
* "I Know Anguish" © 2023, David S. Cohen
* "The Other Prodigal" © 2023, David S. Cohen
* "White Light Baptism" © 2025, Wolf Eberhardt
* "No Hair in the Passenger Seat" © 2025, Wolf Eberhardt
* "INTTYS" © 2025, Wolf Eberhardt
* "Yesterday You" © 2025, Wolf Eberhardt
* "Sleep Walking" © 2025, Wolf Eberhardt
* "Hare's-Foot Clovers" © 2025, Wolf Eberhardt
* "Cactus Conversation" © 2025, Wolf Eberhardt
* "Don't Is the Hymn" © 2025, Jill Spiewak Eng
* "Toast That Screamed" © 2024, Jill Spiewak Eng
* "Swimming in a Thinking Land" © 2024, Jill Spiewak Eng
* "A Hallway of Healing Grace" © 2024, Jill Spiewak Eng
* "A Story Developed" © 2024, Jill Spiewak Eng
* "Miles of Incidental Formaldehyde" © 2024, Jill Spiewak Eng
* "The Dryad" © 2025, Juliet James
* "Ignorant Bliss" © 2024, Juliet James
* "Wicked Words" © 2023, Juliet James
* "Hunger for the Ages" © 2022, Juliet James
* "Frost Scorpio" © 2024, Juliet James
* "July" © 2023, Juliet James
* "kNOw" © 2025, Thomas James
* "Taking It in the Windmills" © 2024, Thomas James
* "Sequestration" © 2024, Thomas James
* "… (Ellipsis)" © 2024, Thomas James
* "A Mending" © 2024, Thomas James
* "Neverfrozen" © 2025, Thomas James
* "Walking With the Dead" © 2023, Claire Kelly
* "Facing the Unknown" © 2023, Claire Kelly
* "Deadly Pace" © 2023, Claire Kelly
* "The Murky Side of the Moon" © 2023, Claire Kelly
* "Par for the Course" © 2025, Claire Kelly
* "Living Dead Lands" © 2023, Claire Kelly

No portion of this book may be reproduced in any form without written permission from the publisher or author, except as permitted by U.S. copyright law.

ISBN: 979-8-9888904-5-4 (Paperback)
ISBN: 979-8-9888904-7-8 (EPUB)

Library of Congress Control Number: 2025942660

Edited by Crooked Circle Press

First Edition

To the giants upon whose shoulders we stand.

Contents

Foreword 1
Jenine Baines 2
    The Audition 3
    Apartment for Rent—No Poets? 4
    Sad Toeholds 5
    Moments & Opportunities 6
    Surprise Symphony from Bob,
    the Music Reviewer 8
    Lift Off at LA Zoo 10

Allisonn Church 12
    How to Exit the Body Gently 13
    Apparitions 14
    Waxwing Season 15
    Waterbird and the First Poem 16
    A Feather 17
    Men invented death but women invented soup ... 18
    The Origin of Wind 18
    Unrequited 19

Doodleslice 20
    Brasso 21
    Fluff and Fold 22
    Recline 24
    Smokestack 26
    I Know Anguish 27
    The Other Prodigal 29

Wolf Eberhardt 30
    White Light Baptism 31
    No Hair in the Passenger Seat 34
    INTTYS 36
    Yesterday You 36
    Sleep Walking 37
    Hare's-Foot Clovers 37
    Cactus Conversation 38

Jill Spiewak Eng............................ 40
- Don't Is the Hymn 41
- Toast That Screamed.. 42
- Swimming in a Thinking Land 43
- A Hallway of Healing Grace 44
- A Story Developed... 45
- Miles of Incidental Formaldehyde 46

Juliet James............................... 48
- The Dryad.. 49
- Ignorant Bliss 50
- Wicked Words... 51
- Hunger for the Ages 52
- The Frost Scorpio... 55
- July... 56

Thomas James............................ 60
- kNOw... 61
- Taking It in the Windmills.. 62
- Sequestration.. 63
- ... (Ellipsis).. 64
- A Mending 65
- Neverfrozen 66

Claire Kelly.................................. 68
- Walking With the Dead... 69
- Facing the Unknown 72
- Deadly Pace 75
- The Murky Side of the Moon....................................... 78
- Par for the Course 80
- Living Dead Lands 83

Foreword

Welcome to *The Crooked Circle Confluence of Poetry, Round 1*. I'm Thomas James.

I've been writing poetry since childhood, but it wasn't until late 2022 that I began sharing my work publicly, on Medium, as part of a personal healing journey. What began as a solitary act quickly became something communal. In the digital spaces of online literary life, I encountered poets whose words stayed with me.

Those writers formed *The Crooked Circle*, which I describe as an individualist collective of structured anarchy. This loosely defined, fiercely talented group of poets is connected by a shared passion for language and truth. This anthology is our first venture into print and serves as a snapshot of creative convergence.

Inside, you'll find a spectrum of voices. Some poems are bold or satirical; others are confessional, abstract, or quietly meditative. There are ghosts here—of trauma, longing, memory—but also joy, wit, healing, and the hunger to transform.

Each writer has provided us exclusively with work that has never appeared in print, and each has included at least one piece never before seen anywhere. Several poets have gone above and beyond the call in offering us nothing but brand new work. Whether you read front to back or dip in at random, I hope this collection offers moments of recognition, resonance, and maybe even renewal.

Thank you for joining us in the circle.

—*Thomas James*

Jenine Baines

Jenine Baines is a retired publicist whose career spanned the performing arts world, promoting orchestras, opera companies, choirs, composers, and soloists. Now, she channels that lifelong love of music into language, writing poetry, meditations, essays, and the occasional spirited screed on Medium and Substack.

Her work resonates with a lyrical sensibility, often blurring the line between voice and verse. Whether exploring the emotional landscape of daily life or spinning metaphor from musical memory, Jenine writes with warmth, clarity, and a touch of theatrical flair.

When not at her desk, she can usually be found at her piano, studying everything from opera arias to show tunes, and she sings as a member of two choirs. Her Substack, *A Septuagenarian Sings!*, is aptly named—echoing the spirit of Ella Fitzgerald, who once said, "The only thing better than singing is more singing."

The Audition

I board a paper boat
nestled beside a waterfall beneath
an imperfectly weeded bed
spilling roses and droplets
of marguerite daisies—
peace lilies peeking languidly
over lichened rocks divided
in opinion
as to whether my craft will capsize

Will my devotions and practice
pay off—my tenor of coloratura
uncloaked, translucent as
the August sky?
Breath effortless
Alleluias soaring
like inverse shooting stars
impervious
to any atonal eddy, rapid, or undertow

Or will a note miss its mark,
a phrase bellyflop back to earth?
If so, may I remember to think
only
that's interesting
as I toss self-recrimination overboard
and continue singing
Voila, my listing boat
with its flimsy thin skin
righting itself
Flowers deliberating, faces unreadable
My own, relieved
Exultant
At least I am trying

Jenine Baines

Apartment for Rent—No Poets?

"One-bedroom apartment. All utilities included. No poets. No smoking." From a want ad in The New Yorker

I get it.
I have trouble cohabitating with Calliope, myself.

She will poke her head
around a corner or, worse yet, force open
the lock on a door—a glittery phrase or two
garlanding her fingertips, her cat-eyed glasses
pearled with prompts.
And while I'd rather take a nap,
water the plants, or paint my toes one hue per nail,
I am powerless.
Yes, it is high time
we get to work, albeit the utility
of our partnership
is questionable.
This sharing
of space is not exactly profitable.
Rejections multiply
like dust bunnies beneath a bed.
Acceptances feed solely
my soul, goose bumped
with dejection.
The rent's too high—
I have wasted my life.
Yet who am I kidding?
I'd be all the poorer, all the more star-crossed
and voiceless if ejected
from her company.

Jenine Baines

Sad Toeholds

"I have lost my smile. But do not worry. The dandelion has it." —Thich Nhat Hanh

Oh, my friends, my mind could use such a good weeding today!

Oxalis and dandelions have plunged their toes
into the loam prepared by my better angels,
whose slim, sleek fingers
are crossed—sparking canticles, rounds, and psalms
while crows watch from power lines.
Their prayer—may green blades of lush joy
weave themselves
into such a tight mat
that illusions release their sad toehold.

Groundcover for the soul.

Turn your back, lower your guard,
welcome at your peril
so much as a mote of despair or distrust,
denial or sanctimony,
self-pity or self-sabotage.
The choker of petechiae
about your throat will tighten.
The whites of your eyes will redden—
karma for your blind repudiation
of Truth.

And yet dandelion distilled
becomes a healing tea.
And how exquisitely oxalis's yellow blossoms
litter the lawn with stars.

Jenine Baines

Moments & Opportunities

I.
Zeus was gorgeous—white fur, blue eyes. A Persian, said the shelter. A breed revered—undemanding, calm, loving. Which Zeus was. Until one morning he strutted into the kitchen and bit me. A bite, no nip.

The attacks continued. Perhaps Zeus missed being outdoors?

Within the hour, Zeus was terrorizing the neighbor's Dalmatian. As I gardened, my ankles grew raw. By week five, I weeded fear. Then, one morning, Zeus wandered off and never returned. Guilt blossomed, variegated with relief. I joke he became the Olympian king of the hill, but I wonder. Then I re-remember. The gods aren't dead.

II.
Ah, the Foreshadowing
life inscribes with sharp claws
on the shredding boxspring of the bed
so prettily decorated
with thick quilts and ruffled pillows
for hiding our heads beneath.

III.
Dreaming
of a blue-eyed, beautiful boy
singing my name, making his way
down the hill to my parents' house.
Decades later
what unsought angel
nudged me awake
at the exact moment
he crooned *I love you too, sweetheart*
to someone else—abandoning me
for a more amenable pet
on a gaslit by-road of blame and steep resentment
sealed with kisses
scented of sulfur and roses
returned to sender and recycled.

Jenine Baines

IV
Again, and again, and again I dare Loving.
Unstintingly, even as my scars still ache
and new ones find their place.

V
The crescent moon tilting like a bell
in an opalescent cathedral
while the mockingbirds,
my morning kettle, and I sing
a communion hymn.

Surprise Symphony from Bob, the Music Reviewer

Though the tree was dead, it spoke to me.
Paint me. Hang crystals from my limbs.

I began, instead, by planting flowers beneath it.
Begonias for gratitude—hot pink
with vitality and grace, bronze-leafed
to better tolerate the sun's daily drenching.

Oh, what deliverance—to be
on my knees,
ridding this world of crabgrass and thistle!
Nestling iridescent seedlings
into freshly amended, sweet dirt.
Watering them in—praising
their pretty pinkness while pondering
what color
to paint the tree rising
like a splayed hand from loose earth.
Pink, too,
or would that be overkill?

I'd settled on lavender
when I learned my great friend Bob had died.
Normally I sing in the shower but, that night,
my throat locked.
The water mourned with me, requiems.

The next morning, I hauled the hose past
the white gaura/whirling butterfly plant
then stopped—awed and entranced
by a surprise symphony of delight.
The dead tree was swathed in blossoms
prismed with dew—peaches,

symbols of immortality.
*Well, my goodness, Bob,
my heart and the green parrots sang.
Tell Haydn hello.*

Poet's Note: *The Surprise Symphony is an orchestral work by Joseph Haydn in which a startling loud chord interrupts the otherwise soft and gentle flow of the second movement.*

Jenine Baines

Lift Off at LA Zoo

"Catch a falling star and put it in your pocket. Never let it fade away."
—Perry Como

Flamingo, my friend,
your luscious pink, black, and white wings lift—
lightly brushing against the musky green fingertips
of the attendant trees

My silver-lined wings cannot help
but spread, too

Shall we stretch our necks and soar
free
of every barricade
then, to the song of the Gibbons,
the laughter of children,
and applause of the seals
make a beeline in a V to the moon,
where we paint it a flamboyant lime?

Our sweet pink webbed feet dancing/our pink beaks dappled with
black, opening

Feeding upon those so-very-precious falling stars
all those blindly earthbound beneath us
fail to catch, put in their pockets,
and never let fade away

Jenine Baines

Allisonn Church

Allisonn Church is the author of *Sunlight Leaking* (Bottlecap Press, 2023) and *Feathered Throat* (Crooked Circle Press, 2025). She was born in a small, rural community to a mother who pinned butterflies in glass cases and hid scarab beetles in her jewelry box. She earned a BA from Brandeis University, where she studied British Romanticism and Russian Futurism. Her work has been featured in *The Hopper, Tiny Seed Literary Journal, Reverie Magazine*, and other publications.

Her poems move with a quiet, reflective grace, folding myth, memory, and earth-bound wonder into spare yet evocative language. There's a quality of stillness in her voice (even when her subject matter is unsettling) that invites the reader to pause and listen closely.

Allisonn lives in Massachusetts with her husband, son, and various rescued animal companions. She spends her days reading, meditating, and discovering poems hidden in moss, feathers, and rain.

How to Exit the Body Gently

I'm tired of trying to appear human.

    Today I will unravel my own skin,
    let the fine mist of a soul seep out;
        I will burst at the seams, an explosion
        of pale gray feathers.

            I will float through open air
            toward the light of a December sun.

Allisonn Church

Apparitions

Each breath of wind
is the ghost of a crow,

invisible body hopping
playfully through grass,

shaking clover,
rustling leaves—

when she ascends
again to the sky,

the whole sky
a host of crows,

the whole sky
empty and full

Originally Appeared in *The Power of Poetry* on Medium

Allisonn Church

Waxwing Season
An acrostic

When branches sway in a March breeze, waxwings arrive to ravage the overripe crab apple. I try to be xenial—letting them feast on the decaying red flesh, watching their boisterous midday meal, camera in hand. I am lucky, for my visitors return every year, and maybe next year they'll remember me; they'll face the window, guzzling up shriveled fruits, flaunting satiny feathers, shielded by black masks as I click frame after frame.

Waterbird and the First Poem

I walk on the beach writing poems
in sand: line break, anaphora,
webbing and claw.

I write for myself, for the joy
of splashing and the brine
of sea snails.

Nevertheless,
those who find my footprints
will tell stories of a bird
who transforms into a goddess,
grants wishes, then vanishes
into night.

A Feather

So rarely
      carried
            away

by wind,

      though it could be—

         any feather from any

            bird.

So fit for   *f l i g h t,*

        for   d r i f t

        and   b r e e z e,

   but mostly, held
      fast

with barb
to flesh.

Allisonn Church

Men invented death but women invented soup

I swirl a slotted spoon through simmering broth and mutter a spell: "O God, to those who have hunger, give bread..." A turkey's dead body floats to the surface. I make it into a charm. The smooth gray ribcage breaks and so, too, do the bonds of hunger: I watch them dissolve into steam, condense against the cold ceiling. My breath mingles with wet death, a gaseous hex, and I pledge to feed the world—return death to life. I remove the bones. What was rendered remains.

The Origin of Wind

Whose breath makes the wind?
What giant cat yawns
beyond the horizon, unseen?
What bird flaps its massive wings,
shaking the sunflower field?

Originally Appeared in *The Crooked Circle* on Medium

Unrequited

The sky feels heavy and
my head feels heavy and
my chest feels heavy and
I can't exactly breathe so
I retreat to my cozy bed
and fall asleep.
While I am sleeping, my bed
wakes up.

To be honest, she hates me:
I am heavy and sad and
my elbows poke her in the ribs.
She bucks and rolls and spits;
I don't sleep well, but
I think it's because my body
is too difficult and too broken
to find comfort. I've never loved
my body, but I do love
my bed.

I snuggle deeply into her quilted folds:
she sighs, harrumphs, grumbles,
tosses me and turns me.
How frustrating for her
that I never read her signals;
that I just keep coming back
for more.

An errant foot catches
on a gash in my bottom sheet and
now I am an animal caught in a trap.
My hungry bed gnaws at the offending limb,
smugly satisfied. I say I'll change the sheet but
I never do. In truth, I never change
anything at all.

Originally Appeared in *The Crooked Circle* on Medium

Doodleslice

Doodleslice is a polymorphously talented, Atlanta-based writer and visual artist with over thirty years of creative experience. Whether on the page or the canvas, his work is shaped by a deep curiosity about the light and darkness that coexist in all human stories. He believes that in the corners of the best fairy tales reside the deepest shadows.

Doodleslice is the author and illustrator of *Color Me With Hugs*, a poetry and coloring book that invites readers of all ages into a whimsical, emotionally resonant world. His poetry ranges from wry and reflective to profoundly tender, often embracing small absurdities to reveal larger truths.

A firm believer in everyday wonder, he claims that homemade chocolate chip cookies are evidence that humans are (ever so slightly) more good than evil.

Brasso

Impregnated wads
Scrubbing into arguments
Sibling squibbling

Presiding in gloves
Good silver and tender nerves
Preparations sulk

Leaves in the attic
Thanksgaving in retrospect
Relative distress

Elbowing eighteen
But one save one less but one
These seats are sagging

Untarnished Montclair
Loud cousins laughing-aching
Shining brassy bright

Fluff and Fold

I am Hans Metterling
Shut-in with starchy shorts
I keep my back to the wall
Neither Gogol
Nor Proust
Ever come for tea
Just as well
One would certainly never leave
And the other would steal my lists

My agent reviles me
It's mutual
He wears bright red socks
I can't abide the excess

Excuse me
Could you put that down?
It's fragile
Thank you
It's an heirloom
Perfectly starched
But brittle
Like my bones
Snapping like pencil tips

I beg your pardon
Go ahead quote me
What should I care?
What passes for journalism these days
A police report
Two and half pairs
Socks stolen
Treasure beyond reckoning
And you want a quote
Pithy
Ad lib
Something spicy
That'll sell papers

Well here you go:
Box or hangers?
Only choosing matters
Unwrinkled vanities
Won't wash away the stains

Now be a dear
And empty your pockets
This is a robbery

Recline

I lay back
Beneath me
Soft earth

I am cradled in dust and grass

I lay back
Beneath me
The Earth

Beyond all horizons
A stone of hope
Immense and patient

I lay back
A child
In this mother's bosom

Gently rumbling

I lay back
My ear pressed to Earth
There are songs there
Buried in industries
Of anthills
And magma

I lay back
Beneath me
The home I will know
I have known

I lay back
Cradled
In earth

Returning
What I have left
What I have borrowed

What a privilege it has been

Smokestack

Treetop smokestack skyscraper
Mountain
There's a limit to how high
A climber climbs
And it ain't the sky
Thin air
We gotta tank for that
But you run outta Earth
Ain't that a kick in the pants
All those rungs
But no more heads to step on
There you are
At the top of the world
Waiting for Gaia
To shove Everest up another inch
You can have it
But you can't go no further
Sitting on top of the world

I Know Anguish

A stranger
Bumped in the hall
Another day
Shared an elevator

We were in the same neighborhood
But not neighborly
My cautious solitude
A rabbit habit

Skittish anyway
Yet strangers wear you down
With polite repetition
And conversational weather

And so the border is crossed
My friend at work
In the grocery
Down a flight

So I've come to know anguish
Through small encounters
My cells, permeable,
Infected

Without contempt
Familiar
Snuffing the candle
Of my joy

The Other Prodigal

I and I I I and Thee
Abide inside depart

Unreturned unhomed
Apart alone

Foresaken

I and I for Thee was I for Thee?
Abound unbound

Asea
Adrift

Jersey diners
Peach pit grift

Father Isaac am I I I
Sacrificed for Thee not I

Abound unsheeped
Wolfishly fat

At that
Less cash

A threadbare coat

Atheist Airways
Have no travel agents

I I I name my own price
Without Thee

The holy land awaits
A ram is still a sheep

Without I I am I without Thee
I I I just I

Without Thee

Wolf Eberhardt

Wolf Eberhardt is a Long Island-based poet whose work spans narrative, abstract, and imagistic forms. A relative newcomer to poetry, he began writing in 2020, but his voice arrived fully formed: searching, contemplative, and unafraid of complexity. Beneath the shifting surfaces of his poems runs a steady current—a quiet insistence on understanding both the external world and the intricacies of the self.

Mythological and philosophical motifs appear often in his writing, not as distant references, but as working tools: scaffolding for inner architecture. His influences include the conversational immediacy of Frank O'Hara, the spiritual gravity of Rainer Maria Rilke, and the intimate irreverence of e. e. cummings. That blend of introspection and play gives his work a unique emotional frequency—equal parts lucid and haunted.

Wolf's poems often feel like internal monologues mid-transformation. They arrive unfinished only in the best way: inviting the reader to witness thought as it becomes feeling.

White Light Baptism

White is the color of purity
Of rebirth and renewal
And there you stood in it with a slowly sinking sun grazing the back of you as I looked into your eyes
I don't know what language they speak but I understand it all too well
White is the color of purity
And of letting go

In my car with the slowly sinking Sun on my windshield
I noticed a small spider web
First I saw it in the right corner those lines like highways
And I kept scanning the landscape and through some intricacy the web made it all the way to the left side of the dashboard
Moving through every leap and bow and trouble along the way
And I have to decide what it means
And nearly in the center hangs a dark hair with hints of red

And now I look outside of my car window
There's a web, where it curves between the ceiling and the wall of the car
And in the air is floating a bunch of particulate I'm not exactly sure what it is
Perhaps pollen
And one of those spores for my dandelion before it becomes a dandelion just flew toward and then upward over my car
And the pollen is entering
The sun has gotten lower since I saw you for what is probably one of the last times
It is quiet
It is warm
The wind has died down
And maybe I'm okay, but I've lost my spark

(continued...)

Wolf Eberhardt

White Light Baptism *(continued)*

Against the late afternoon sun
You stood there in all white
The color of purity
It ran and curved along your body
And the dark of your hair contrasted with the intensity of the look in your eyes
Or maybe it wasn't intensity
Maybe tragedy is the better word
It pierced through me
I'd like to be able to tell you how beautiful you looked despite the sadness
I'd like for things to have been different

So you hand me my sweatshirts that I leant you
We met each other's gaze
And we held it
Everything that could have been said had been said
Everything that could have been felt... Well I don't know
Not when you feel it in person
And it has been a long time since we saw each other in person
There's tragic and then there's tragedy
There's sober and then sobriety
What sins does one commit to have what they want?
What level playing field is there for those who break the rules?
Maybe it is too late to have the answer to that

It's much easier to understand the sin than the sinner
And it does not always mean that it's evil
It may mean that it complicates life
Two asteroids took each other on a trip
They found each other in orbit
And let themselves be carried by it
Despite
Everything

Wolf Eberhardt

I look up, a couple is walking their baby
You don't see that much anymore

We're divorced and we aren't even married
If white is the color of baptism in fire
Then we can destroy all of this
For how you looked cannot be replicated
And how we looked at each other cannot be replicated
And I would not believe that there was a more complex space that exists in the universe than what existed between our gaze
Despite its short passage
There are no words for it
But you looked very nice in all white
Like you were on your way to be reborn
And to leave all this behind

I've made a mess of your expectations

Wolf Eberhardt

No Hair in the Passenger Seat

An archetype sits in bed beside the open window
Fresh snow lays around as an ocean
Moving with the wind
The wind
Its sound is the howling of whispers
Dressed in black
I feel things die in the turn of the year
The snow
It's sound is the muffled renewal
No-thing yet said
Encapsulating potential
It may melt away
Melt away like
You
When I think back
It was Autumn
Most surely it was
I remember the crunching leaves and the harsh wind
And how you seemed to me like a Spring child learning the world
The winter kills all
You listen to what the wind is trying to say—
Nothing

They're unthought things
At least, they were
Is it the same for you? We've not spoken in a long time
And I was willing to keep them unthought and merely experienced
Is that Dasein?
But something seems to have grabbed me and shook me
I think it is the solitude of a winter night with distractions cut away
A forcing to feel

What could I do for you?
It was never enough
How many tries would it take?
There were far too many

And by some strange cruelty I've not even been able to find any of your hair in my car
And against all expectation
And despite the wayward travels
I've not been able to find a single hair of yours
In the passenger seat
Believe me, will you?
I looked
And there's no reason for it
No excuse
I've looked
And searched
Maybe you really are gone

INTTYS

i need/to tel/usome / thing that''''''' S onmy/ind
ndit looks as i/yes do (that
n it cntrcts in a BRIGHT light/s all r(ounding mecannot see hea)r
touch or feel or brush against
my death
n|i need/too tel/usome / thing that '''''''' S onmy/mind
if/i/// st u t t
ered it/s onin(preparationofyourtongue
not purpose there is/n'''''''t a −way>(((out)))
wh/at/c/an itellyou/   impasse
a way in (you say clearly with weird words

Yesterday You

Yesterday you
Laid on me and tears came down your face and dropped on my pants
Yesterday you said you hate me
Last night you kissed me
And we were drunk and we rolled around and wrestled in the grass, laughing
Last night you said you love me
Last night you called me beautiful and told me goodnight on the phone
This morning you told me that you have to let me go
And never said another word.

Wolf Eberhardt

Sleep Walking

It's not for style when I put my worst foot forward
It's not for nothing when I burn things into the wind
And let them go
It's for the greater morally questionable when I accept impulse
For one knows that suffering could be worse

My feet
Oh my feet
The past I'd left
I thought I outgrew you
My feet
Hug the rim of an old canyon

Dreams
Dreams only mean something if they're understood

Look
There is an indent where I slept the night prior
This is something that I cannot outgrow
I put the blankets back in place
I put my worst foot forward

I dream—I hope that I come back with all that I've come for

Hare's-Foot Clovers

That interstice between where you start
and I begin
Somewhere lay Infinity
Sleeps on a belly of Hare's-foot clovers
Erupts from your robin's nest head
In a garden of Even
Balance of I and you
Feel it too

Wolf Eberhardt

Cactus Conversation

After a strong drink the wall of trees start dancing their leaves. They twinkle under an afternoon sun in May and all I've written before is wrought iron. How should I do it now? I've grown distant from my eyes and from jumping lines. It's the age of the prosaic and disorganized thought. Imagine if I could talk for hours.

There is soil and there is sand and very rarely can vegetation take hold in the sand. Some vegetation can. You know this; you've seen it. Survivors. Keep them. YHWH don't like ugly. God don't like ugly. And I've learned that purity is the natural state and decay is what sin is. So there's sin in death, even in those plants dying in the sand. And that is why when Christ rose from the dead and then ascended to Heaven, that is why He is without sin. It's far too late for you. Ego can't come roundabout without some sin. But you can't remember your first and who knows if you had a choice. You probably didn't have a choice. But God don't like ugly. You're ugly; always will be. They say Christ came down to save us. Show God we arnt ugly. Deserve to be saved. An' imagine a desert without plants. Death valley about. Ugly as all hell. You get a plant strong enough to survive it and grow on you then you keep them close because they're vouching for you like Christ vouched for us.

All right. Were God not troubled he may be bored. Life is trouble. Monks have no fun. They may die and nothing happens. Might as well have fun. If no one's stranger to sin, God may smite you either way. You've read the wrath in the Old Testament.

Old Testament is an introduction to the new. That was a godless world. Saw glimpses they did. The man on high was not here. Damn near took a virgin to bring him down. Joseph never did cut his hair like Samson. Understand? Truth is sometimes hinted at—there ain't nothing that'll replicate the truth though.

So Christ saved us. Doesn't that mean we can sin all we want without consequence?

Damn if I know. Far as I see it you wouldn't want to. I seen men go about in sin all through it and they ain't never find happiness. Never. Yeah they get high. It ain't a stagnant joy. The sun's bright on Monday. Or Tuesday. Or Sunday. But the other days is all new moon. Livin' for the little light they know but ain't workin' for what they could find. Maybe the cactus is flawed too. Maybe it's gotta be to grow in a desert. It ain't about replication, it's about livin' right 'cuz that's the forest or nice plains.

The wind picks up and the leaves aren't just glistening now
They are dancing
The hair dances over the forehead tickling it
Or itching it
They scratch
There are ways to say things and ways you cannot say things
Some lose a lot
Some lose too much
Does the sun rise higher if you wait?

Jill Spiewak Eng

Jill Spiewak Eng is a poet, essayist, and mindfulness educator whose work blends the intuitive and the intellectual. A longtime author of philosophical and self-inquiry-driven nonfiction, she developed Mindful Reality, a body of work that validates who we are and what we do through a non-dualistic, deterministic lens. Her recent poetic voice has taken a more abstract turn, crafting prose poems that reflect mindfulness, grief, memory, and the rhythms of lived experience.

Her poems fuse personal history with universal questioning, touching on topics such as emotional trauma, naturalism, impermanence, relationships, and recovery. Her stream-of-consciousness style owes inspiration to Gertrude Stein's *Tender Buttons*, and carries echoes of philosophical inquiry and emotional unearthing.

A former professional modern dancer and certified Alexander Technique teacher, Jill also holds a master's degree in international relations and communications, and she has lived up and down the eastern U.S., calling Maine home since 2001. She is a mother, grandmother, and lifelong explorer of the inner and outer worlds.

Don't Is the Hymn

Ending a smile made the scenery cumbersome in its likeness. Some of a date went away to stillness. Calling embers confined into traveling imperception. Delicate dials flapping wind in disguised colors.

You appear in dreams of change. Alluring sediment of natures distant. A wonderment wondering who was where. What, compared with form, in other. Pictures of people of songs that ring.

Pulling. Grafting adhesions lingering seems to be familiar in pose. Heavy wanting alit with fumes dancing and disappearing. Caution and play with offers missing stay. Decisions absent to give enough of a plea.

Chants against repeats forgotten as life. Doubting the casting of eyes in depth. Gone as a willow unfurled. Beating wild in patterns subsumed. Taken of that for a stance chiming turns.

Don't is the hymn. A cave under pain. For not consumed breath. Chilly with grief. Destined to ground unadorned of a search. Complete as a token engraved down below. Lasting sounds shimmer light emphatic in tone.

Toast That Screamed

Most in a cup to rinse what is found sends a piece of cake to taste. A grin of soup poured from the night shines a style of salt that is moist.

Can it know for what has been seen the noise of cream with a glass-structured frame? I pause, to delete, when beknownst to me is hidden upon the feet beneath.

Toast that screamed a holler of loss inside the grasp that shaped the sweet. I caved to date unless the charge was more than a streak that sang me to sleep.

A disguise I admit however the state you misspoke again leaving me crushed. I deflate and leave the kitchen of delight no matter the treat offered at best.

Will it be a thing to behold and swallow when all along the table turns? Is a draft again a way back in to the oven that cooks the meat and pie?

I wonder aloud in thick and thin if might and peace go hand in hand. A shake of powder with smells so bright concocts a flavor I'll never resist. A scene of relief or a final goodbye.

The dance goes on behind the curtain with snacks on the side to float the suspense. I spot a trace of missing crumb on the floor outside the sliding doors.

Do not believe I can abide with sugar and spice that isn't nice. Honey perhaps if stirred just right I'd consider to give a second chance.

Originally Appeared in *Write Under the Moon* on Medium

Swimming in a Thinking Land

once in the distance of a nearby seem was a reminder of how it might be. coming up in short as an awakened stance of wondering. taking what is known to appear from the shape of an inkling.

watching it wander in the mentality of a season. swimming in a thinking land that dives deep into wanting to know. how a future will unfold. emptying to guess at suppositions.

and nothing travels from a place of impossible speculation. the mystery lies ahead in second-hand passings. images pronounced in sincerity of clarity. still is the absence of informative calculations.

shake a tree to see a piece of earth show its destination. like the beat of a foot in a direction of spontaneity. just to the rhythm of actuality. the sudden claim of distinct metamorphosis.

a change of a scene in depths of surprise. connections stemming from signaled insistence. must is a now for the weight that imparts. creative installments slipping through the grains of everyday life.

Originally Appeared in *Catharsis Chronicles* on Medium under the title "Watching It Wander"

A Hallway of Healing Grace

In, for the static of a mere shape paused the taste of breath. Trapped with centrifuge, a pillar inside discourse could no longer handle change. A channel broke the wave sending signals downstream toward patterns lost.

A sounding board left what was once a place of restoration. Walking away crept beneath shadows grieving distance. Darkness lit up the new hallway of healing grace. Peace was found inadvertently without a wink skidding backwards.

Stanzas of growth gravitated in sideline directions. Shooing this way and that decided on patents with novel understanding. A breathtaking view admonished historical landmarks. There was no need to return.

A lost cause refrained leaving shallow footsteps in mud. A story bled for memory. Dampened temperatures flew wings into graveyard semantics while connections were chewed away by time. Steam rolled into far-off bed springs.

Coming to terms released acceptance into relief. Slow buds popped from dead land. Delicate pacing converted a chase to a pause when tiny increments smiled at freedom. Capability set ease to levels unrecognizable.

Originally Appeared in *Write Under the Moon* on Medium

A Story Developed

A roof and a sound, water to run, with a noise under there, touching eyes for the moments of heard secrets. Room for something blending a portrait together with making a life into perhaps ways of being.

Sorts and desires, a field playing news, for the run of, in between types and differences. A brief win toward announcing what lingers as good. Accents coming loud when what was discovered sat forth. Home created there taking ground.

Proof of now gone to then. Flickers lit, by ago and streaming around to the beat of amorphous parts inside waking semi-ports. In. Of the nature for that which speaks seemingly quiet watching a space entering a mere speck.

Import. Seeing must and receiving this about a near call dropping few with finds of happening attributes. More. The knowing not, having a thing poking through blanket ideas deleting scenes. Messaging units turn a move after another.

Would, and the wind has a spot showing a drift inclined. A general statement imposes form to areas misinterpreted beneath agreement. I never knew the amount of what came to be. A story developed leaving loss.

Originally Appeared in *Write Under the Moon* on Medium

Miles of Incidental Formaldehyde

a jump of poison turns a stomach into a missing headache. sunshine falling into a decrepit plot of incremental destitution. tipping underbellies sending feet to distant shores. miles of incidental formaldehyde smelling stones against what is known.

on the floor beneath carpets is a push toward fragile steel. aching nights dealing upon witchy hunts to mean what is happening. hyper hints tearing pieces into dirt. a wish is a death is a feel is a collapse. nowhere can a rose live under a boulder rolling.

trapping infinity accords rightful glares. commercial acceleration sends cellos to clouds of fury. reaching light steers echoes into chambers. imperceptible nerves mourn treasures deleted from how to live in a world.

reason and distinction, a memory of trial and error. contorted pain supposed with nearby malfunction. ragged runs deciphering mistaken glory. unbearable loss curves balls thrown into the sky. trains wrecked toward silent nights.

pretend care styled against sense. waving dissection brought forth to annihilate creative habitation. while a life breathes fresh air, dust patterns lungs beneath arterial circulation. veins bleed into tracks pleading for survival.

Originally Appeared in *The Crooked Circle* on Medium

Juliet James

Juliet James, author of *Cravings: A (Mostly) Fictional Memoir* (Crooked Circle Press, 2025), is a queer, bisexual, fat writer whose work explores memory, identity, resilience, and the quiet ferocities of everyday life. A current MFA candidate at Bay Path University, she brings a keen anthropological lens to her writing—unsurprising, given her background in anthropology from Hunter College. Her poems often blend personal narrative with cultural observation, creating work that is both emotionally intimate and socially aware.

Originally from New Jersey, Juliet spent formative years in New York City before settling in the mountains of Colorado, where she lives with her husband, fellow writer Thomas James, and their beloved dog. Her work embraces selfhood in all its contradictions, and she writes with tenderness and clarity about bodies, relationships, and what it means to be seen.

When she's not writing, Juliet enjoys road trips, loud music, and collecting stationery she swears she'll use someday. She names her houseplants and, with varying degrees of success, keeps them alive. She believes in fat joy, chosen family, and the sacred act of telling the truth—especially when it's hard.

The Dryad

There's a forest in here, she says
as she reaches into my chest cavity
Peeling back the bark and revealing
the wood pulp beneath
I expect her to pull out my heart
bloodied and red
Instead, she pulls out Spanish moss
Strand after strand, vibrant green
Spongy
It has taken comfort in the humid warmth
of my body and it has flourished

Ignorant Bliss

She says, people do say ignorance is bliss,
When he tells her, more information
is always better than less
Not agreeing with the sentiment, but rather
pointing out why others push back on
his idea
Silently, I think, my brain befuddled by sleep and
sickness, that I miss that bliss
The haze of unknowing
And wonder again why I've worked
so hard
Carefully pulling apart the fragile, sticky layers
A bitter baklava of trauma
that never ends
And the only thing my
Exhausted brain can think in reply is,
You deserve to be whole

Originally Appeared in *Iceberg's Poetry* on Medium

Wicked Words

Words are weapons I have not always wielded wisely
There are things I would unsay
Words that were not untrue, but not true
To who I am
Betrayal made me reckless, using words
Without worry
Wounds aching, wanting retaliation
Words whipped out with wanton abandon
Careless with my serpent's tongue
In moments of wild rage
Wanting to stop my pain but
Hurting myself far more than I
Would ever hurt them

Originally Appeared in *Voiced Verses* on Medium

Hunger for the Ages

13, and craving my first kiss
My peers so far ahead on this road to adulthood
I can no longer see them beyond its curves
Lost and left out, I walk it alone

Then... friend of a friend
Classic would-be bad boy at 14
Our first kiss an awkward dare, a joke I am not in on
Until after, when it's dissected by him with
my friends, and declared DOA

It was like licking an ashtray, I tell them,
determined to publish my own necropsy of
this monumental moment gone wrong,
to be read by the friends and the boy who played me

When he asks, I let him be my first boyfriend
There are no other applicants to consider
He will cheat on me before the month ends

15, and bored
I call a pay phone in the
McDonald's parking lot
Boy with a cute voice answers, and we talk

He becomes my next boyfriend
First to take any care for how he makes my body feel
Second to break my fragile heart
He gives me no real reason for our abrupt parting
The girl he takes to homecoming a few weeks later
is thin

17, reverted back to 13
You'd be so hot if you only were thin, he says, unsolicited
But his hands map the curves of my 300 pounds
in spite of this declaration that becomes a refrain
As he threatens to devour the essence of me, and I let him

Juliet James

When I starve my body in
futile attempts to make it what he wants,
he ironically tries to feed me
On a balmy August evening, I tell him I'm hungry
But the food is bland,
and I am still so very hungry
For something I have not yet tasted

19 to 21
So many men want to feast on me
If only behind closed doors
One kisses me for two hours, then asks me to be his
first lover
My friends can't know, he adds
They wouldn't understand, he says, as he gestures to the body
that he wants to be his undoing

But I am not 13 any longer
I've started to see my own worth
I'll pass, I say,
As my heart throbs from the familiar pain
of being too much

22, and ready to abandon the idea of love
Finally, I've learned
Using bodies can work both ways,
and I do not hesitate to play their twisted games
Determined to not fall again

When I meet my epiphany
He tells me nothing of my beauty
or lack thereof
Instead, he tells me I seethe

(continued...)

Juliet James

Hunger for the Ages *(continued)*

Beneath his hands, I feel what he sees
As my body brews with a heady concoction
His pentagram necklace, relic of a past life,
makes me believe in orphaned dreams

He takes in all of me;
brain, being, and body
The same one deemed too much by others
Feels cherished by him
I find quiet in his arms
He tastes like home, comfort food for my careful soul

He will challenge my heart as I slowly change his
I am nothing if not persistent
and I do not lose easily
The night he finally says, I love you
I know that
He is who was always missing

46
And we still travel life's
perilously beautiful roads together
My hunger fully satiated
But I still crave forever in his heart

Originally Appeared in *Scribe* on Medium

Juliet James

The Frost Scorpio

I try to remember her apologies, ones that were for me, not herself
Surely they must've happened
But I remember nothing that felt real

Letting your child abuse you and others isn't making amends
But she tolerates his behavior anyway,
No matter who he hurts

It made me sad for her until I saw that damage reflected
in yet another child she professes to love
Then I seethed to know another generation will suffer

I scorched the earth because I needed to cauterize my wounds
I tried too many times to reach past her icy exterior
Only to get my heart frostbitten

Originally Appeared in *The Crooked Circle* on Medium

Juliet James

July

July is East Coast childhood and roaring 20s,
my great-grandmother giving me fresh off-the-vine tomatoes,
rinsed with a garden hose, that I eat like they are apples,
seeds and salty-sweet juice running down my chin
Ice cream Sundays with my father and little brother at Frosty Freeze,
Soft serve strawberry ice cream cones and, hurry, eat it before it melts

July is no school, be home when the streetlights go off freedom
And days spent with fair-weather friends in my grandfather's pool
It is sunburnt skin and stifling humid nights conspiring against sleep

July is sitting on the pool deck, watching illegal fireworks, the scent of sulfur heavy in air that crackles with electricity
It is turning down impulsive marriage proposals that could only end
In heartbreak and tears, though not necessarily mine

July is my father's mother, her seemingly infinite strength inspiring me, even as I fear her impatience and sometimes sharp tongue
It is spending a stolen teenage summer night sleeping on a beach with a close friend
It is getting lost with another friend while the Gin Blossoms play on the
radio, in a time before GPS or Google Maps

July is summer days down the shore,
fresh lemonade, frozen custard, boardwalk pizza
And fingers sticky from the powdered sugar of fresh zeppole
It is burning my bare thighs
On the metal of sun-heated rides and benches

July is my terrible first kiss
A first boyfriend
And the ruby-red haze of lust and love
It is learning new tongues that teach harsh lessons
needed to tell the difference between that which feels good
And that which truly is

July is American Spirits on the 4th,
Lorenzo flirting, and Iris playing—and a drunken promise to never fall
in love with him again,
My buzzed brain basking in its brilliance
Thinking, I can promise this since I never fell out of love
And knew I never would

July is Real Feel 106 degrees at an unexpected Saturday street fair in NYC
It is MozzArepas and grilled corn on the cob, husk used as a handle
Makeup melting off my face, mascara burning my eyes
Buying bootlegged Ani CDs in a West Village record store
The blasting AC almost too cold, yet a wonderful relief

July is the end of six months of interminable waiting
When he finally says he loves me
Weak knees, stomach fluttering, grabbing the kitchen counter
For support
Trying not to drop my cordless phone
Because I knew, but wasn't sure he'd ever admit it,
Even to himself

(continued...)

July *(continued)*

July is my last new boyfriend.

July is sweltering summer days, Central Park fly fishing, and convincing myself it was cooler
In a rowboat on the lake where we lingered for hours
It is ponderous clouds swollen with rains they will not release
Heat lightning and distant thunder a tease
Praying to an unanswering god for relief from the endless heat

July is Colorado adulthood
Rocky Mountain summers
Wildflowers weaving a living tapestry of
vibrant colors over mountain hillsides
Humidity 9 percent instead of 90
Homes without AC because it isn't even needed
(Or wasn't not even two decades ago)

July is naked mountain tops and aspens undulating in alpine breezes,
Peridot leaves shimmering in the sun of a short summer respite
In a land where winter's sparkling snows reign supreme

July is monsoon season
Afternoon thunderstorms a guilty thrill
As I comfort our frightened little dog
Wicked winds and lightning bolts
And anxiety-inducing red flag warnings
When the monsoons leave

July is beautiful places with too many people
It is Bison, Bears, and Banff
Gushing glacial streams of otherworldly hues
Alongside a road named for ice
Though the day is in the 90s
It is holding his hand over the console of
Libby, Gina, Veronica, or Betty

July is my least favorite month,
Never a fan of heat or bugs
But a midwinter's dream
Showed me that I am not unlike July
Unruly and chaotic
Unpredictable and complex
Quick to spark with anger, but just as quick to weep
Ready to start anew while knowing there are no fresh starts,
Not really
Even as I try to shove the heat-warped doors on the past closed
Once and for all

July is a reminder that all is intertwined,
The storms, the sun, the heat, the rain
All are needed to grow
And I am ready for that
Finally

Originally Appeared in *Voiced Verses* on Medium

Juliet James

Thomas James

Thomas James is a poet, editor, and founder of *The Crooked Circle*, an online literary magazine dedicated to showcasing emerging and unconventional voices. Though he has been writing poetry since childhood, he returned to it in earnest in 2022 as part of a personal healing journey. That return became a path of connection—first with language, then with a growing community of writers who now comprise the Crooked Circle collective.

His work often explores philosophical inquiry, emotional survival, and the surreal edges of belief and meaning. Both playful and precise, his poems blend lyrical inventiveness with a hint of formal experimentation. His style was heavily influenced early in life by J.R.R. Tolkien, Lewis Carroll, Edgar Allan Poe, Shel Silverstein, and Dr. Seuss.

Thomas lives in Colorado with his wife, Juliet James, and their devoted dog companion. When not writing or editing, he can often be found thinking about the future of poetry, working on one of his many aquariums, or planning a road trip, whether or not he's going to take that one.

kNOw

To accept an idea is a slippery slope,
and to reify thought a most perilous course.
If belief is a gateway to frivolous hope,
let us cut off that dream at the source—
with alacritous, purgative force.

Once the con of a concept is let through the door
like a vampire unwisely invited to tea,
things can never return to an empty before
that was truly and foolishly free.
Sticky thoughts are not things one can flee.

May the metaphors melt in your mouth and disperse.
Don't let notions take notes in indelible ink.
Though to learn is a boon, to be sure is a curse;
the assumptions can change in a blink.
Never know when, instead, you could think.

Thomas James

Taking It in the Windmills

My ability to reconstruct reality around me is unique, and that astounds me every time another can't. I manipulate the weave into whatever I conceive, and I assume it, though the evidence is scant. The hype of a hypothesis, the burn in the esophagus—I charge like a rhinoceros, just following my nose. I trip the light quixotic (the effect is self-hypnotic). I don't know it's idiotic 'til the close.

There are futures I can nearly see; they're hovering in front of me and whispering a guarantee if I can just believe. When no one sees the giants, then I focus on compliance with analysis and science, and I grieve. I take it in the windmills, all the mountains and the molehills; just a wish awash in unrepentant, cold reality. I accept what I can't change, and then I start to rearrange surviving facts into a novel phantasy.

Originally Appeared in *The Crooked Circle* on Medium

Sequestration

My neurons spark like faulty wires.
My flashbacks rage like forest fires.
My paranoia's grippy tires
can drive while upside-down.

The terror birds are hunting still.
The vampire bats have drunk their fill.
The ghost sharks live in lightless chill
and simply will not drown.

Volcanic bombs that fall like rain
and seismic waves I can't contain.
The eyelid of my hurricane
is open, far and wide.

The lines across my aging face.
The carvings in this dusty place.
Unfathomed canyons ever trace
great rivers that have dried.

My musings are itinerant,
explosion always imminent.
When shrapnel harms the innocent,
I suffer tenfold pain.

Enclose me in an airtight room.
Discard me in a leaden tomb
so deep that no one might exhume
this cataclysmic brain.

Originally Appeared in *Blue Insights* on Medium

... (Ellipsis)

I threw my voice
and heard it break
against the stony silence.
I chose a choice,
and thus I spake
with tongues of hungry flame.
Lament, rejoice,
and come what may,
no scheme or deft contrivance
can hope to hoist
a colorway
to extirpate the blame.

If, through my voice,
a hush becomes
vernacular and thingly,
then empty noise
and wordless mums
will bloom throughout a fall.
Dead air employs
the benefit
of slipping through so thinly
that quondam joys
can't follow it
through such a tight-knit pall.

Originally Appeared in *The Crooked Circle* on Medium

A Mending

Sing me a dirge in the houses of healing.
Cracked to the core, and the lacquer is peeling.
Slips of the mind redefined as revealing
by Argus-eyed sentinel shades.
Wail like a banshee foreshadowing nothing.
Waitlessly dire and yet tardily crushing.
Pearls of false wisdom are perfect for clutching
while cataracts blur the cascades.

Open like wounds from a past with no future.
Knit back together with exigent suture.
Granting new rights to an authorized user
who's broken the system before.
Watching and waiting for virtue to vanish.
Sanguine security seems Pollyannish.
Eager for evidence ample to banish
the fog of a previous war.

Eyes on the prize with peripheral peril.
Bird in the hand, but its instincts are feral.
Doubt is contagious, yet pretense is sterile
and lacks the potential for growth.
Hard-bitten hide that is thick and resilient.
Adding agility now would be brilliant.
Chasing my tail while pursuing fulfillment
of sober and sacrosanct oath.

Originally Appeared in *Blue Insights* on Medium

Neverfrozen

Sands of time, the grains are crashing,
wrapped in glass awant of smashing.
Falling earthward, wailing, gnashing;
crystal moments, clumping, clashing.

Breakers whitecap stormy weather.
Beaching, teaching, rockrose heather.
Bird in hand and bird of feather,
then and now, and altogether.

Sink a stone and skip a season.
Fill a void devoid of reason.
Perfidy, thy name is legion.
Trust is requisite to treason.

Pinned between the wabe and gnomon,
thunderous like fate or omen,
swelling as the open ocean,
everchanging, neverfrozen.

Claire Kelly

Claire Kelly writes from the quiet spaces between life and death, dream and memory. Her poetry has a steady, unmistakable rhythm—gentle yet resonant. Through vivid imagery and a fluid sense of time, she explores what lingers in the shadows: grief, longing, and the surprising resilience of hope.

Her work has been noted for its emotional depth and subtle, unexpected turns of phrase. Rather than following conventional patterns, her poems often drift into places that feel both familiar and strange. The result is a voice that feels intimate yet distant—thoughtful, searching, and deeply felt.

Outside of her own writing, Claire is the editor and curator of *Write Under The Moon*, a literary publication on Medium and Substack. There, she supports emerging and established writers alike, bringing the same care and sensitivity to their work that she brings to her own. Whether writing or editing, she remains committed to exploring and elevating the quieter truths that connect us all.

Walking With the Dead

Iron sides,
fallen factory lines,
fools gold dims the sun's mimes
and mimics imprinted footprints as moving time,
but fossils magnify perceptions
becoming present inside themselves,
and all battered oars bleed their own blind spots
before cutting waves into yesterday's oceans
that seep into man-minded lands
with seashore sand at a glorious price—
you can't stay without paying the tolls
with small slices of paper mache
and one heart set to boil underneath oblivion.

Soil burns past black
shovels churn in bittersweet toil
as roots dig deep to drink days of life,
and the echos plant seeds that sprout past leaves
that blow with the breeze to appease
a stagnant air that inhales ghosts
who lie firm and maintain the motions—
do we dare to just stop?
and think about sight sideways
or upside down and in between?
or stay with fitted ways,
since ancestors agonized over eyes
sized to see without sway.

(continued...)

Walking With the Dead *(continued)*

Decay breathes
manufactured laws of life
into buildings
that hover in their own structure,
but with a heartbeat
pulsing into malnourished minds,
and built inside dusty black or off-white ideas
encased in frames of the past,
now a monument of precious things
to preserve at a collection of costs—
and that's where I saw you
beyond melted memory form,
your shape ebbing into dawn
your face looked worn,
a translucent hazard
carrying embers of sacrificed shards,
your eyes tall and torn
from all the things
you could never let go
to hold.

Then I saw me,
almost alive,
but halfway before dead,
my past versions never waning,
never almost abating
until I grasped the present
and watched it become
a palpable point of no return—

(continued...)

it's a good thing I have a retired ruby-red dress
that suits any ongoing occasion,
like a date with death,
maybe a visit to the old diner
that exists on both corners
of every lane with every name,
or for going round and round
on tours of every city I've been to
before now,
and after
I dipped my head
into islands of you.

And so it goes,
repetition binds,
history repeats
into pinpricks of disguises,
while words gift-wrap truths
with plenty of pretty colors and bows
and plenty of voices vocalizing each other,
marking appearances as changed—
but under your wristwatch
time stopped,
once the secondhand
made it past two shades after nine
as clouds twist the same sky—
so I stopped to ask why
to the dead man walking,
to the dead man ringing broken bells,
and to the dead man with the relentless face
whispering tired reasons to tall trees
to keep singing the same unending seasons—
but they all just looked right through me,
as if I were the ghost.

Originally Appeared in *Imogene's Notebook* on Medium

Claire Kelly

Facing the Unknown

Lately
you've been trying to tell time
by reading a clock
you can't see
but you feel its presence
weaving itself
into your heart
beats

A pounding
pulsating
echo chamber
that takes
seconds
to combust
every minute and hour
into rusty dreams
of man-made
ticking machines

You can now hear
everything you touch
the sounds splinter
and clash
into one
spinning
form
of familiar

After years of
overdone catastrophes
it's time to demolish
any fleeting notions
that you can change
the direction
of the waves

Claire Kelly

in an ocean
that was already
set into motion
long before you decided
to dip your toes
into its vast expanse
while cursing
your human tomb
because
the salt burns
your ancient
wounds

You're on fire
peeling off layers
of frazzled
frenzied
illusions
that you can stop
the sun from setting
even when you know
it can't deny
the call
of the moon

You're now
a reflection
surrounded by
endless mirrors
that echo
what is
you

(continued...)

Facing the Unknown *(continued)*

But you're
blinded
by that pale
hollow
face
still encased
in flesh

that bleeds
with the pulse
of the earth
and it has you grasping
at moonlight straws

The night air
breathes
its slow movements
into a glance
you can taste
the letters
that form
as they grasp
at your tongue
leaving nothing
to chance

You become the dance
when you no longer
decorate the darkness
with your
temporary
circumstance

Originally Appeared in *Scuzzbucket* on Medium

Deadly Pace

You were always moving so fast
from day one
when you lunged out of the glorious gate—
head spinning
bones twisting
muscles begging
for mere minutes of mercy
always yearning
for anything
a speck of something
for one more hour in the day
just one more luscious kiss on strange lips
before they all became distant dewy shadows
of the unlisted lovers who ran off
after showering mutilated affections
with nothing more to say

Even for just one solid night
maybe you could convince the silky static sky
to shoot stars in your deadened eyes
and show you every single thing
you've been dying to see
since before everything felt like nothing
and before you wove single threads
into a million patterns of dedicated dread

(continued...)

Deadly Pace *(continued)*

You wanted to turn into plumes of silver dust
and float into every pinhole of infinite blackness
then spin into everything inside of yourself
and stay tangled in the songs
that sang your dreams into decades of shady blues
to learn why you found such chaotic reasons
to fly into fields of golden doves
and fertilize wilting flowers of bitterness
you continued to chase
all the way to the dark side of the moon
before they died from view
and before you realized you could
set yourself free
from all the limitations
of temporary conditions

Then the voice
it rumbled in the misty air
it flowed in with the sunrise
and ebbed inside the tiniest tides
while snapping in echoes of deep throaty tones
vibrating through your core
a core you forgot you knew
and stalled your spinning with one fatal blow—
he said you won't last
everything you know will come to pass
this pace is deadly
even when you're seamlessly constructed
from scorching hot flames
to fuel you through
decades of self-hatred
and blame

As the wars of your thoughts rage on
you keep marching in a straight line
dying to go on and on
while you know that time ticks for no one—
slow down before your feet combust
and your bones decay into filthy piles of anger-infested debris
breathe in and don't forget to blow smoke signals
before your shiny exterior collapses
into the emerald vastness
of artificial green grass turfs
that will outlast you
and your last legacy

As you lay on the earth's floor
slashing the sky with open eyes
your words will drown
into simple sputtering sentences
of self-defeat
and you know it's time
time to go inside
time to sit with yourself
face your hawk-eyed demons who demand your view
make friends with how they tread in your thoughts and hack your mind
and let them slice your days into bites you can digest
you can't change what's out of your hands
you don't control this spin
you never owned these lands

Originally Appeared in *Write Under the Moon* on Medium

Claire Kelly

The Murky Side of the Moon

11 pm
the avenue lights buzz from flying in dim,
cobwebs bow to no whims under misty encores
as windows frame eyes on the streets
and fall into pace with walkers who exist unnamed
and line the construction of night—
I'm far from my mind,
farther from my trimmings,
evolving then suffocating
stifled inside the monotonous haze,
disputing pieces of myself I lost to the days
when my thoughts patterned themselves
blind and filthy from every other plight,
when they weren't my halos to hold
only solo spotlights
and what about seeing my own sight?

Now I'm just here,
floating these feet across the road
stumbling on coercion
that forms cement-caressed cracks,
none of it ever speaks to anyone that's me
it all just echos with the train tracks
to blister a devil into the distance—
I get lost in the tides of metal
grating creation from the land,
an isolating journey of engines
and dusty fuel-born lows
never abating
into the longings of times and places—
and so it all goes
dicing through the atmosphere,
it never stops and it never drops dead
until you leave it as it lies
with words stuck in unsaid.

Claire Kelly

I feel parched from the daylight,
I feel ripples recoil
etching the murky into the moon—
and it's nights like tonight
I can somehow see my shadow
sinking stars into seconds of skies
trying to find where I am losing volume,
and it's all filtering my gaze away from soon
giving way
to the murky side of the moon,
the kind of murky where things aren't quite anything,
not quite new,
not quite blue,
not quite any forgotten color-coded hue.

I heard it happens when the moon hangs
low enough
to drink away all casual certainty,
but now I can't hold you in my hands
since you slipped through my skin
then faded into the blackness of tomorrow's sky,
and my instant view
imploded yesterday afternoon—
that's the murky side of the moon.

Originally Appeared in *Write Under the Moon* on Medium

Claire Kelly

Par for the Course
wreckless abandonment

A midnight
shed
into
days of dead
scraping tar
from humanity
vs.
humans
fixated on
passive
overdrive

I
burden
my
miles
propped
by splintered
scrolls
born from
willful disregard
for the human at stake

caution now
a lake died

oblivious as creatures of the grind
yet craters exist
in this Roman winter
while we feast
on
fruits of the slaughter
fruits of the fraught
rattling ribs
for nickels and
dimes

what crimes?

systems glitch
but systems go
I was never born to run
under
one
hollow ground
where mighty spawn falls
where no bells toll
where no whistles blow

Is there any escape
from our hellscape pact?

shiny things to distract

yet my pauper feet
milk bones
whether I speak
blame
or whether I will
rage
inside the horrors
under a black sun's
five-alarm fire
beyond Brooklyn
boulevards
and hazy
fades
of family lines

(continued...)

Par For the Course *(continued)*

when witches
were painted
wretched ones
while cloaked ones
painted their own wings
our blended societal bleed
strictly transactional
empathy
derelict

now
a crime to
feel
is
the time to
tis the season
for treasonous tears
WE
islands of one
moats of many
repetitive reels
of time

Living Dead Lands

You have yourself
always did—
instead you keep digging
into your picked-over pocket full of terrors
for calculated currencies of errors
but how about two pennies for your thoughts?
such costly gazing gadgets
never on sale as priceless
what about knowing your mirrored mind
and where your heart pumps its bleeding binds?

You now notice
your white footprints draw black flames
you didn't even realize it snowed—
white powdered roads
settle you into a winterized cage
and you're tired of waiting beyond fall
your cold bones rage and seasons change
without opinions or reasons
forcing you to release
load-bearing loads

They say the city never sleeps
but it's dying
it's already dead
it already melted into living dead lands—
did you check its pulse?
did you speak it into sweetly stale lies?
did you watch it seeping souls slowly
into pristine jars trying to breed lives into control
like sludge simultaneously cementing the streets
under an old clock with maddening chimes
that never speaks sometimes?

(continued...)

Living Dead Lands *(continued)*

You always feel naked
thoughts buried yet bare
but your exhausted legs
so lusciously long
with tight jeans and ripped seams
echoing your pace with red leather and broken lace
making sure you were seen but not watched—
images never erased
black tie events about faced
but those days weren't about your heart
and now the bucket is empty
blindly broken and already used
pretending now eludes

You can smell the hungry beast
with your calloused eyes
but you can't see it surmise
that you can't get lost in the city of empty lies
when you realize you were dead
long before you arrived

You lay on your back
scanning lonely skies for seedling stars
but street lamps impale your mind's eye
all you can see is gore
the smell of green grass elopes with the trees
the tide long turned artificial
automated
and autotuned
a festival of machines

It's all just become
cities that seep salty years
bleeding gold and frantic fears
as you bellow your horror into the night
screeching your alien veil into new light
always alone
you wish for home
to take you back—
blackened skies answer all whims
nature is as near and distant as the dark side of the moon
it all beckons you close
it beckons you to think
with your very own
beautifully faulty
forsaken mind

Originally Appeared in *Scuzzbucket* on Medium

Thank you for reading!

If you'd like to keep up with what we're doing, you should follow us on Medium, subscribe to us on Substack, and join our mailing list to be informed of future projects. You can do all of those things from one place:

https://www.thecrookedcircle.com

www.ingramcontent.com/pod-product-compliance
Lightning Source LLC
Chambersburg PA
CBHW060405050426
42449CB00009B/1908